Original title:
Chlorophyll Confessions

Copyright © 2025 Creative Arts Management OÜ
All rights reserved.

Author: William Hawthorne
ISBN HARDBACK: 978-1-80581-728-4
ISBN PAPERBACK: 978-1-80581-255-5
ISBN EBOOK: 978-1-80581-728-4

The Verdant Veil

In a garden of green, where secrets hide,
A leaf told a joke, the trees all sighed.
The grass wore a grin, though roots were quite sore,
Claiming it danced, but tripped on the floor.

Beneath the bright sun, the vines set the stage,
Each petal a player, in nature's own page.
The daisies all giggled, the roses had fun,
But the thorns rolled their eyes, 'We're outshone by none!'

Open Book of Blossoms

A daffodil spoke to a shy little bud,
"Don't worry, my friend, you won't turn to mud!"
With laughter and petals, they plotted quite bold,
To prank all the bees, and the blooms manifold.

They painted the lilies a bright shade of blue,
While tulips threw parties, inviting a few.
The flora conspired in harmony's tune,
As the daisies declared, "We'll be back by noon!"

Dappled Truths

A sunflower boasted of its lofty height,
While gossiping shadows watched till the night.
The ferns whispered secrets, quite cheeky indeed,
"The trees may be grand, but we're all they need!"

The acorns laughed heartily, deep in their shells,
Making up stories like clever little elves.
In the heart of the woods, where laughter was rife,
Nature's own comedy, a hilarious life!

The Allure of Arboreal Lies

The oaks told tall tales of their own grand affair,
Claiming they danced with the wind in the air.
But the willows just chuckled, with roots in the ground,
"We've seen all your antics, you're not so profound!"

A squirrel piped up with a nugget of cheer,
"The best of the jokes, my friends, is right here!"
As the leaves fluttered, the laughter took flight,
In their verdant domain, all was merry and bright!

Nature's Confidential Chronicles

In the garden, secrets grow,
Plants gossip more than we could know.
A daisy says, 'My petals are shy,'
While weeds claim they touch the sky.

The bushes chuckle, sharing a root,
Saying carrots wear big radish boots.
Trees gossip about the breeze's sigh,
While squirrels sketch plans for a pie.

The daisies dance under the sun's glare,
But at night, they braid each other's hair.
A tulip whispers, 'I'm out of tune,'
As the moon peeks over, jolly like a balloon.

Nature thrives on jest and jesters,
Roots and stems, they're all the testers.
When the flowers meet for evening tea,
They laugh at how wild they wish to be.

The Art of Leafy Lies

Leaves tell tales in a swirling breeze,
About a snail who thinks he's a tease.
"I'm the fastest!" he shouts with glee,
While others munch on just 'leafy brie'.

A cactus claims it's a prickly star,
While succulents dream of being bizarre.
Ferns wave their fronds, "We dance with grace,"
While moss settles low, a cozy embrace.

Pansies pout with colorful flair,
"Just look at us, we're the ones who dare!"
Petunias paint their petals bright,
While the lilacs hum in pure delight.

Oh, the garden's filled with leafy lies,
Where each plant wears its own disguise.
In this world of green and cheer,
Everyone's smiling, that much is clear.

Green Shadows of Identity

In the shade of the mighty oak,
The ferns plot pranks, oh what a joke!
"I'm a tree!" yells a tiny sprout,
While the daisies blink, filled with doubt.

A leafy vine claims it's quite the star,
As it stretches, just a tad too far.
In the dark, the shadows argue and play,
"I'm more rooted, say what you may!"

A mossy stone shares ancient rhymes,
While brambles weave their twisting chimes.
The daisies blush, finding their way,
As they whisper secrets, bright as the day.

In the patch where the wild things grow,
The grass chuckles low, putting on a show.
Each shadow has tales of its own,
In this garden, no plant feels alone.

Whispers from the Woodland

In the woodland, tales intertwine,
A squirrel claims he's a wise old sign.
"Ask me anything, I know it all!"
While mushrooms giggle, having a ball.

The owls hoot secrets in the night,
While crickets chirp with all their might.
"I saw a fox wearing a hat!"
"Those silly tales, imagine that!"

Beneath the boughs, stories unfold,
Between each leaf, whispers bold.
An acorn dreams of reaching heights,
While fireflies flash their dazzling lights.

In this funny forest of glee,
Even the roots join the mystery.
Each tree is a storyteller at heart,
In the woodland, laughter's a form of art.

Green Tales of Regret

In the garden where I tried to bloom,
I tripped on roots and met my doom.
The daisies laughed, what a silly sight,
My grass stains glowed under the moonlight.

I watered weeds, thought they were great,
Turns out they're just my twisted fate.
With every snip, I made a mess,
Now I'm the queen of the wilderness!

My plants have secrets they won't share,
Who knew ferns could gossip with such flair?
As I prune with care, I still don't know,
Why my lilies decide to steal the show.

Next year I'll plant with a bit more grace,
Perhaps I'll let the daisies have their space.
But here's the twist, they'll surely die,
Because houseplants are just too shy.

The Shade's Secret Song

Underneath the leafy veil so wide,
Lies a chorus where the critters hide.
Squirrels boast of acorn feats,
While the shadowed flowers hum with beats.

I danced along, tripped on a root,
Laughed with a worm in my garden suit.
The sunflowers waltzed, the daisies twirled,
Oh, what a funny, leafy world!

The breeze chuckled with every sway,
Tickling grass, guiding ants at play.
In the cool shade, secrets unfold,
A comedy of nature, bright and bold.

And as I sat there, dreams in sway,
I wondered if I'd ever find my way.
Maybe tomorrow I'll pick a new spot,
Where none can hear my laugh—oh, what a plot!

Sprite's Shade of Lies

In the willow's grasp, tales start to shift,
That cheeky sprite, oh what a gift.
Crafting stories, making me believe,
This cheeky shade knows how to deceive.

"I'm a flower!" it gurgles with glee,
Wearing petals that no one can see.
As I chuckle, it starts to pout,
A playful trickster, that's what it's about!

It whispers tales of roots so tall,
While jesting leaves begin to fall.
Innuendos flutter, giggles abound,
Do sprites get in trouble? Not on this ground!

So beware the shade that seems so fair,
For laughter hides in every layer.
Nature's whispers weave a silly game,
And the sprite just dances, never the same.

Flora's Unveiling

Flora stepped out in her lovely attire,
A dress of petals, all bright and dire.
The bees all buzzed, so intrigued by her sway,
And the sun's bright kiss sent the shadows away.

With a wink she flaunted her leafy crown,
While cheeky vines tried to pull her down.
"Twist and twirl!" the daisies cheered,
But Flora laughed, "That's not what I feared!"

In the middle of this leafy hall,
She realized her blossoms stood proud and tall.
But when the twirling got too intense,
She tumbled right into the fence!

With petals askew and a smile so wide,
Flora's laugh had nowhere to hide.
She whispered soft secrets to the bumblebees,
In a garden where giggles sway on the breeze.

Conflicting Green

In a leaf of emerald hue,
I thought I saw a clue,
But it turned out to be,
A rumor from a tree.

The grass had quite the chat,
About a gossiping cat,
Who claimed to know it all,
Yet tripped at every fall.

Each shade told tales of woe,
Of sunburns and the snow,
While vines wrapped round their dreams,
And whispered silly schemes.

In the end, we all agree,
We're green as we can be,
But laughter shared out here,
Leaves our worries disappear.

Shadows of Shaded Thoughts

Underneath a leafy roof,
Where thoughts twist and goof,
The shade holds secrets tight,
While crickets chirp with delight.

A dandelion dreamed of flight,
In such a silly plight,
But when it tried to soar,
It settled on the floor.

The willow weeps with glee,
For humor's like a spree,
As laughter nests in knots,
And wiggles with the thoughts.

Under these twisted vines,
Where laughter intertwines,
We're all just evergreen
In this funny green scene.

The Heartbeat of the Grove

Beneath the bark, a pulse does thrum,
It echoes fun, not just the hum,
Of leaves that shake and sway,
In a rhythm of the day.

A squirrel once took a chance,
And joined the branches' dance,
He twirled and spun with flair,
Until he lost his hair!

Under canopies so wide,
Giggles have nowhere to hide,
Every root has got a joke,
Like trees that love to poke.

So come and join the groove,
Feel the heartbeat, make a move,
In this forest full of cheer,
The joy of green is always near.

The Guilt of Greener Pastures

Oh, the grass can be a tease,
With hues that aim to please,
But every blade just sighs,
When guilt begins to rise.

"I should have known," the flowers moan,
While confessing all alone,
That they looked across the fence,
And their green was much more dense.

In pastures lush, with giggly sheep,
Who plot and scheme, then fall asleep,
They dream of lawns that gleam in spite,
Of their own little plight.

Yet every overcrowded plot,
Turns gossip into rot,
So let us now embrace,
The fun, the guilt, the green space!

The Confessional Grove

In the greenwood shade, secrets grow,
Whispering leaves put on a show.
Trees giggle softly, while squirrels plot,
A mishap with acorns, oh what luck they've got!

Mossy confessions on a bark-smooth stage,
Bunnies hop gossip, it's all the rage.
Sunbeams peek through, casting a grin,
While the wise old owl rolls his eyes with a spin.

Fungi sit snug, listening in tight,
Chiding the daisies for acting all bright.
Funny little beetles trample the scene,
Spilling the tea on the grass so green!

So under the canopy, laughter's the rule,
Where each secret shared becomes a joyful fool.
In this grove of mirth, with nature so spry,
Confessions bloom open beneath the blue sky.

Secret Gardens of the Soul

In the hidden patch where wild things roam,
Laughter seeds sprout, calling it home.
The flowers sway to a giggly refrain,
While worms tell tales of the recent rain.

Shy violets flirt while daisies declare,
That yesterday's sun was beyond compare.
Gnomes stand guard with grins oh so wide,
Whispering gossip of bugs that collide!

A rogue tomato sneaks into the chat,
Boasting of size and a sneaky leaf spat.
The hedges all chuckle at the clumsy deer,
Who trips on her hooves, we laugh, can you hear?

In this garden realm, the humor flows free,
With every bloom bursting with foolish glee.
Secrecy thrives in this playful expanse,
Where nature's light heart leads the dance!

Melancholy of the Meadow

In the meadow where dandelions sigh,
A ponderous breeze floats lazily by.
The grasses gossip, yet feel a bit blue,
Because the blooms insist they're prettier too.

Butterflies flutter, high drama in flight,
Claiming to be stars in their meadow delight.
Yet the crickets croon in their nighttime choir,
Beneath the moon's glance, they never tire.

A melancholy bumblebee wears a frown,
Hesitant to visit that floral crown.
While the poppies tease him without any shame,
His pollen-packed dreams are never the same!

Frogs gather round, sharing laughter and woe,
With riddles and puns only they seem to know.
In this meadow of moods, both funny and deep,
Nature's own laughter is the secret we keep!

Shrouded in Shade

In the leafy lounge, I hide,
Disguised from sun, my leafy pride.
The neighbors think I'm quite aloof,
Yet here I am, just goofing off.

The squirrels laugh as they pass by,
I plan a party, oh my my!
With acorns stacked and branches spread,
We'll dance and twirl, no fear, no dread.

A shady charade, oh what a plot,
With vines and twigs, we've got a lot.
The sunlight beckons, 'Come and play!'
I'll stay right here, it's my best day!

So if you see me poke my head,
Among the greens, do not be misled.
I'm the life of parties, can't you see?
Under this shade, I'm wild and free!

Blooming Awareness

One day I woke to blooms around,
A flower's giggle, such a sound!
They whispered secrets of the earth,
Of bees and bugs, all full of mirth.

"Hey you! The green, with quite a pose,
Don't you know how it feels to grow?"
I chuckled back with leafy flair,
"You're just here for the garden fare!"

Petals flutter, colors dance,
In this garden, we take a chance.
I tried to blend, but oh so bright,
Each bloom a joke, what pure delight!

Amongst the petals, I found my way,
To laugh with blooms throughout the day.
They tease me so, but I don't mind,
In this patch, true joy I find!

Unveiling of the Green Veil

Behind this veil of emerald sheen,
I've secrets hidden, yet unseen.
A dandelion's bold complaint,
"Why must I be the court's old saint?"

I play the part, in shades I dwell,
With roots so deep, can't cast a spell.
But hear me now, just one good joke,
I'm king of greens, hear my wild croak!

The sun will shine, the breeze will wail,
As I emerge, I'll tell my tale.
Of garden gossip, flower fights,
And creeping vines on silly nights.

So let the laughter fill the space,
As we unveil with leafy grace.
What fun awaits when green is bold,
In this secret world, new stories unfold!

The Inkwell of Leaves

In the inkwell where secrets blend,
Leaves scribble tales with a twisty bend.
I pen my thoughts in shades so bright,
A storybook of leafy delight.

The wind provides the perfect page,
While sunbeams add a giggly stage.
Each rustle tells a playful tease,
As I draft my tales with utmost ease.

Amongst the words, I lose my way,
In the ink of green, I laugh and play.
With whispers soft, I weave my prose,
Of clumsy bugs and wiggly woes.

So gather round, come hear my lore,
Of dappled light and leafy floor.
In this inkwell, my heart is found,
With every chuckle, joy abounds!

Nature's Hushed Secrets

In the garden, plants whisper,
Secrets held in silent veils,
Roots tickle earth, laughing gently,
While the sun lends golden tales.

Butterflies dance, they gossip light,
About the blooms that steal the show,
Petals blush, in colors bright,
Nature's drama, a sweet, slow flow.

Grass blades gossip, oh so sly,
About the bee that comes to sip,
With winks of dew, they can't deny,
Life's a wild, wobbly trip.

With every rustle, there's a jest,
The trees laugh, as squirrels play,
In nature's realm, we are a guest,
Taking in the leafy ballet.

Meeting of the Moss

In the shade where soft things grow,
Moss convenes for a grand debate,
Who's the fluffiest? Oh, we know,
Fungi joins, declaring 'I'm great!'

A snail slides in, joins the fun,
"Let's not forget my slow-paced flair!"
They giggle, poking fun at the sun,
"Too bright! We simply can't compare!"

Lichens laugh, they cling with glee,
"No one can match our perfect blend!"
While whispers travel through the tree,
Nature's squad, no need to pretend.

As shadows dance, they share a cheer,
Each tiny world, a story spun,
With laughter louder than they appear,
The mossy meeting just begun.

Sons and Daughters of Decay

In the heap where life's tossed away,
Worms wiggle, holding a grand ball,
"Who knew we'd thrive in such decay?"
A fest of fungi, hear the call!

With scraps of laughter in the air,
They twirl in rot, so proud and spry,
Nutrient sprites, without a care,
In muck and mush, they all comply.

Old leaves cheer, they know the score,
They break down fast to feed the new,
"Who knew we'd be the earth's great chore?"
A cycle spins, forever true.

In the huddle of woe and grime,
Beauty blooms, as laughter plays,
Sons and daughters dance in rhyme,
Finding joy in the soulful ways.

The Glimpse of Growth

Tiny sprouts poke from the ground,
With giggles soft, they herald light,
"Look at us! We've finally found,
A way to reach our dream so bright!"

Buds are whispering, blooms appear,
"Watch me stretch, I'm growing tall!"
In visible laughter, nature's cheer,
Each leaf a story, each stem a call.

Roots do a jig beneath the earth,
"Hey, look at all the space we need!"
In comical roots, they flirt with mirth,
Finding fun in the life they feed.

As petals yawn and shake in glee,
Nature's humor, alive and sly,
In each glimpse of growth, we see,
Life's silly dance will never die.

The Roots of Resolve

In the garden of dreams, I dig my feet,
Dancing with daisies, what a funny feat.
I swear the weeds whisper their secret advice,
But they only suggest I should roll like a dice.

With every new shoot, I waddle and sway,
The worms throw a party, they sing and they play.
I ask for their wisdom, they just laugh and squirm,
Roots are for holding, not making me firm.

A sprout in the sun, with a crazy big grin,
Thinking it's clever, oh where do I begin?
I try to stay grounded, but they lift me above,
It's hard to be serious when I'm covered in love.

I trip on the stalks, and I tumble with glee,
Roots may be steady, but they're also quite free.
So here's to my journey, amidst all the blooms,
Life's not just vibrant—it bursts with costumes!

Surrender in Seasons

Spring brings me laughter, with buds all around,
But summer's the joker, it jumps up and down.
I lie on the grass, with bees buzzing near,
Do plants really laugh? Oh, I have my fears!

When autumn arrives, I'm swept in a swirl,
The leaves do a tango, a colorful twirl.
But winter, oh winter, you chilly old chap,
Wrap me in snowflakes while I take a nap.

I try to adapt, but the seasons are sly,
One moment I'm dancing, next, I'm just shy.
The sun gives me kisses, the rain brings me jokes,
Yet here I am giggling, pretending I'm folks.

I roll with the changes, embrace every hue,
For life is a painting, and I'm just a view.
Through laughter and leaves, let my spirit be free,
Surrendering seasons, come laugh at with me!

Mossy Meditations

On rocks where I ponder, the moss starts to chat,
It shares tales of bugs and the adventures they've had.
I sit there in silence, lulled by the green,
Those tiny debates, so profound yet so keen.

With each squishy step, I start to transport,
Into a world where I'm not just a sport.
The toadstools giggle, the ferns flirt and sigh,
"Meditate with us, don't just pass by!"

I hear them discussing the best place to grow,
As I join the conversation, my worries just flow.
"Who cares if I'm human? Let's just play like kids!
In the heart of the forest, that's where life really is."

So let's cozy up, let the moss be our guide,
In this squishy retreat, there's no need to hide.
With humor in nature, we giggle and grin,
Meditations in moss—a laugh from within!

The Illusion of Infinite Green

Oh, the grass looks green from a distance so fair,
But once you get closer, there's patches, I swear!
With clovers that giggle and dandelions that tease,
Nature's a prankster, oh how it aims to please!

I took a quick jog in the midst of a spree,
A tumble and roll—now, look at me!
My shirt's painted green; I'm a walking cliché,
Did someone just shout, "Nature's here to play!"?

The trees stand tall, but they're leaning askew,
I swear they're tipsy on their favorite dew!
With branches that wave and some leaves that applaud,
They're all having fun, oh how they're so odd!

So don't take it serious, let laughter be seen,
In this wild, chaotic, illusion of green.
Join in with the plants, let their craziness flow,
Life's a grand garden; let's embrace the show!

Leafy Reveries

In the garden, whispers sprout,
Leaves debate what life's about.
One says, "I'm the best at shade!"
The others laugh, their hopes displayed.

A sprig of mint joins the talk,
"Freshness wins, let's take a walk!"
They pose and preen for passing flies,
As daisies roll their knowing eyes.

The tall grass speaks of height and fame,
"Not all can bask in sunlight's flame!"
A rogue weed cackles, "I'm the champ!"
While daisies dance like nature's lamp.

With every breeze, their secrets flow,
To the tune of nature's funny show.
The leafy crew, with glee, confides,
In merry chats where humor resides.

Emerald Echoes

Beneath the boughs, the laughter swells,
Roots share tales, their secrets tell.
"My veins are green, I'm bold and brave!"
Scoffs a fern, "I'm quite the wave!"

The mossy stones snicker and gleam,
"Life's a blanket, let's all dream!"
While vines entangle their gossipy ways,
Whispering jokes through sunny rays.

Buds burst forth with giggles bright,
"Who can outshine me in the light?"
A sunflower chuckles, tall and proud,
"Stand back, I'm the talk of the crowd!"

Amidst the greens, a playful plot,
Nature's jesters, never caught.
With laughter woven, roots entwine,
In leafy echoes, fun's divine.

Conversations with the Sunlight

Sunlight beams, with cheeky rays,
"What's your plan for sunny days?"
Said the petunias, bright and bold,
"We're here for gossip, truth be told!"

The daisies chimed, "Let's bloom and chat!"
"We'll whisper secrets, imagine that!"
While shadows play a gentle hook,
In the dance of light, let's write a book!

Basil winks with an herbaceous tone,
"I've got jokes that are all my own!"
Cilantro laughs to keep it cool,
"In this garden, we're nobody's fool!"

As beams of warmth wrap trees in glow,
They share their dreams, they ebb and flow.
In sunny circles, jokes emerge,
A leafy laughter, a vibrant surge.

The Songs of Green

In the forest, where silence sings,
Leaves create tales, on emerald wings.
A sapling whispers, "I'm a star!"
While others giggle from afar.

Broccoli joins, with a crunchy grin,
"I'm tough, let the fun begin!"
The ferns reply with a soft sway,
"Life's a comedy, hip-hip-hooray!"

Tall oaks share their age-old lore,
"Back in my day, we danced with more!"
While seedlings chuckle and do a jig,
In the songs of green, they find their gig.

Nature's choir, in harmony,
Creating tunes, oh, so carefree.
With every rustle, joy takes flight,
In the canopy, laughter ignites.

Messages in the Leaves

In the trees, secrets sway,
Whispers from branches play.
A squirrel nods with glee,
Saying, "Come climb with me!"

Frogs are crafting their own songs,
In the pond where nature throngs.
Lily pads groove with flair,
Choosing tunes beyond compare.

Every leaf a letter sent,
From flowers that are well-bent.
Petals chuckle in the air,
Sharing jokes beyond compare.

So next time you stroll on by,
Listen close, give it a try.
Nature's humor's not a trap,
Just a giggle gap-to-gap!

The Language of Ferns

Ferns in whispers talk and tease,
Flicking fronds in playful breeze.
In their shades, a dance unfolds,
Telling tales that never grow old.

A tumbleweed rolls with a laugh,
Joking 'bout the plant life path.
Dancing on the wild terrain,
Where roots make friends with the rain!

Their jokes are green and spry,
A leaf flips under the sky.
"Why did the bark go out at night?
To find some fun, that feels just right!"

So lean in close, lend an ear,
The foliage has tales sincere.
With laughter mixed into the earth,
Nature's humor shows its worth!

The Secrets of Sprouted Souls

Underneath where sprouts dwell deep,
Dreams arise from nature's sleep.
Worms dig dirt with a silly grin,
"Let the planting games begin!"

Tiny seeds with hopes so wide,
Start to sprout, they cannot hide.
"Why so serious?" they quirk and jest,
"Being green is simply the best!"

Grasses giggle as they sway,
In sunny light, they dance and play.
Roots exchange their silly puns,
In the dirt where laughter runs!

So when you gaze at greens around,
Know they're laughing, so profound.
In every bud and blossom's role,
Lies a secret sprouted soul!

Shades of Deception

In the garden, tricks are bold,
Petals painted, tales retold.
Daisy dons a shiny mask,
"Guess my name, it's quite a task!"

Cacti offer prickly hugs,
While sunflowers pull sneaky shrugs.
"Who's the tallest in the lot?"
Very few can guess the plot!

A vine whispers, "I love to climb!"
But every twist is quite sublime.
Those who peek may find a jest,
In the shadows, green's the best!

So when you wander through the blooms,
Watch for laughter hidden in rooms.
Every leaf a tale will tell,
In nature's tricks, all is well!

Rituals of the Rainforest

In the jungle, the parrots prance,
Wearing hats, they lead the dance.
The monkeys swing with cheeky glee,
Conducting symphonies from a tree.

The frogs jump in their tiny shoes,
Choosing colors like they're in a snooze.
A sloth yells, "What's the fuss today?"
The leaves shake it off and sway away!

The jaguar joins with a purr and a grin,
Underneath, the wiggleworms spin.
Each critter has their own quirky way,
Celebrating life at the end of the day.

Each rain drop seems to cheer and clap,
To the beat of nature, they take a nap.
The breeze giggles, the vines intertwine,
In the rainforest, everything's just fine!

Shade's Embrace

Beneath the boughs, a turtle snores,
Dreaming of pizza and open doors.
A squirrel mocks with a nutty jest,
While others play cards, just like the best.

The shadows chuckle and weave around,
As critters in capes leap off the ground.
A chameleon teases with every hue,
Claiming, "In my world, I can be you!"

With a wink, the vines start to sway,
Like they're off to a party, hip-hip-hooray!
The leaves gossip in a rustling tone,
"Oh darling, your outfit is all your own!"

The sun peeks through with a cheeky beam,
Turning every puddle into a dream.
In this embrace, all just seem to vibe,
Reflecting nature's fun-loving tribe!

The Leaflet's Lament

A leaflet sits, all wrinkled and flat,
Complaining about the weight of a cat.
"Why do I bear this furry friend?"
"It's a burden, but hey, I won't pretend!"

A gust comes by, lifts it with flair,
"Hold on tight!" cries a bug in despair.
"This wind is wild, making us twirl!"
"Just enjoy, my friend, give it a whirl!"

They spin and laugh, then come to a stop,
Amidst the laughter of the raindrops.
"I may be tossed, but I feel so free,"
"Who knew life as a leaf could be a spree?"

With a chuckle, the sun breaks the gray,
Leaving shadows of worries to play.
The leaflet grins, embracing the sun,
"Turns out, life's better when you have fun!"

Fable of the Forest

In a glen, the wise owl would say,
"Let's gather 'round and share our day!"
The hedgehogs giggle, the rabbits chime,
As they swap tales, creating rhyme.

A fox tells a story, oh what a hoot,
Of how he once danced in silly boots.
The trees sway softly, joining the tale,
With whispers of laughter in the breeze's gale.

A deer steps forth with a twinkle in eyes,
"I once wore a crown made of thistle pies!"
The mushrooms chuckle, their caps bobbing high,
"Queen of the forest, give it a try!"

But as the night drapes its velvet robe,
The critters hum their nighttime lobe.
With every fable shared and spun,
In the heart of the forest, they're forever one!

Harvesting the Hidden

In the garden, secrets grow,
Napping gnomes, they steal the show.
Tomatoes laughing, peas in sight,
Dance away from morning light.

Rabbits plotting under shade,
Pests no longer feel afraid.
Carrots whispering with the breeze,
They claim they're all just trying to tease.

Pumpkins boasting of their size,
"A little squeeze, we'll mesmerize!"
Herbs join in the silly fray,
"Let's throw a party, hip hooray!"

With every seed, a tale unfolds,
A garden giggle, laughter bold.
So gather round, the plants agree,
Harvesting fun, for you and me.

Revelations of the Root

Underneath the soil so deep,
Roots confide, their secrets keep.
They gossip 'bout the weather's flair,
"Watch out for squirrels, they love to stare!"

Carrots chuckle at the beets,
"Who's wearing red? We all have beats!"
Radishes blush with a cheeky grin,
"Let's jazz it up, let the fun begin!"

Snakes slither past, with eyes so wide,
"Who knew the garden had so much pride?"
They twist and turn, in muddy socks,
While ivy learns some TikTok knocks.

Laughter bubbles through the leaves,
"Why worry much? Nature believes!"
In roots we find a vibrant hue,
Secrets shared by me and you.

A Lament of Lushness

Oh, such green, but where's the thrill?
"Too much water? Who's had their fill?"
Ferns are grumbling, grass feels sore,
"Can someone please open up the door?"

Vines get tangled, a lost ballet,
"Twirling's hard when you can't splay!"
Flowers pout, "We need some sun,
This humid hug just isn't fun!"

Yet there's a sprout who sings with glee,
"To grow so tall, just wait and see!"
So while we wail at leafy woes,
A lesson blooms where wild laughter grows.

In every plight, a joke will come,
Like slugs in shells, all feeling glum.
Nature's jest, a jumbled cheer,
In lush lament, we find our sphere.

Oxygenated Dreams

Breathing deep in green embrace,
Plants remind us of their grace.
"Exhale worries, inhale cheer!
We're here to spread joy, never fear!"

Photosynthesis is the game,
"Sunshine's glory, don't feel lame!"
Even cacti dream of rain,
"Just a sprinkle, rockstar fame!"

In a pot, a curious vine,
Spying neighbors, "Is that a line?"
Lettuce wisdom, crisp and fresh,
"Keep it cool, don't feel enmeshed!"

As the breeze brings tales to share,
"Float on scents, without a care!"
In dreams of oxygen, we scheme,
Flora's laughter, life's a dream.

The Green Veil of Honesty

In my leafy guise I jest,
With every breeze, I'm put to test.
Lies fall like dew on grass so lush,
Yet here I stand, a green-clad hush.

Critters gossip, they can't keep still,
Whispers echo with every thrill.
"Who's the biggest?" they chuckle, grinning,
I hold my ground, truth's just beginning.

With vines entwined, I hold my claims,
Grass stains on my honest games.
Funny how the sun lights all,
While shadows giggle at my call.

So raise a toast with roots of cheer,
In this garden, we know no fear.
The truth will sprout, just give it time,
In this grove, we dance, we rhyme.

In the Embrace of the Wild

In tangled limbs, we tell our tales,
Of daring blooms and verdant gales.
A squirrel pranced, with acorn crown,
Shouting secrets, laughing 'round.

The bushes rustle, sharing lore,
Of hidden quirks behind each door.
I blush in green, in wild delight,
As laughter twirls with day to night.

A fox in fray, a cheeky grin,
Mischief lurks beneath the skin.
Nature's drama, a comic play,
In every leaf, a joke to stay.

So sing along with nature's crew,
With roots so deep, we'll laugh anew.
In this embrace, let giggles sway,
As wild as green, we find our way.

Beneath the Boughs of Truth

Underneath the wise old trees,
Secrets swirl upon the breeze.
Beneath my bark, I chuckle low,
With branches swaying to and fro.

A wise owl nods, "Life's just a joke,
The lighter moments are what we stoke."
With leaves that rustle, I proclaim,
The silliest truths are fair game.

The sunbeams tickle, shadows tease,
In this leafy laughter, find your ease.
Come gather round, your worries shed,
Under my shade, we'll laugh instead.

In nature's court, we share a jest,
Those boughs bear witness, at their best.
So join me here, where humor thrives,
Beneath the truth, our spirit strives.

Songs of the Swaying Saplings

Little saplings dance with glee,
To the tune of a buzzing bee.
They sway and sway, with roots secure,
In the melody, they find their cure.

The breeze whispers sweet, "Just be bold,
Share your secrets, let them unfold."
With giggles shared in leafy cheer,
Every twirl turns whimsy near.

"Oh look at me!" one shoots so high,
While others laugh, they try to fly.
Their branches wave in playful jest,
A sprouting band, they're simply blessed.

In this garden, joy's the key,
As saplings sway, we're wild and free.
Let's sing aloud, our voices blend,
In every note, our laughter extends.

The Conflicted Essence of Green

In sunlight's glow, I bask and beam,
Yet curse my job, it makes me scream.
Photosynthesizing with glee,
But laughter's worth is hard to see.

With leaves so bright, I dance and pout,
My friends say 'leaf it, just chill out!'
But rooted here, it's quite absurd,
I'd trade my stem for just one word.

The bugs all stop to take a snack,
But hey! I want my greens back!
In gusty winds, I sway and sway,
While squirrels steal my peace away.

So here I stand, with roots so deep,
In this green life, it's hard to leap.
But merging laughter with my shade,
I grow in jest and never fade!

Verdant Memories Unchained.

Oh how I miss those summer days,
When sunlight played in wild displays.
I used to roll, grow tall with pride,
Now I'm just foliage worldwide.

I've grown with shades of envy green,
While pondering just what could have been.
A leaf with dreams is still a leaf,
But can it laugh, or just feel grief?

I catch the breeze with leafy wit,
But fairy tales don't quite fit.
To dance in rain or cheer for bees,
I wonder if they'll share with me.

Still, here I sway beneath the sky,
In whispered thoughts, I surely sigh.
But every breeze brings joy anew,
With all my friends, life's quite the view!

Verdant Whispers

I whisper secrets to the breeze,
While playful critters climb the trees.
A vibrant green, I hold my ground,
Yet laughter echoes all around.

The ants parade, they march in line,
In tiny hats, they think they shine.
But oh, the sass, I just can't cope,
I cheer them on, it's my only hope.

While flowers giggle, shining bright,
I roll my leaves in sheer delight.
They call me 'green,' yet I am wise,
With leafy thoughts and quirky ties.

So join the fun beneath the sun,
In tangled vines, we laugh and run.
Each day's a jest, we twine and play,
In leafy life, we seize the day!

Secrets in the Canopy

In the tall trees, secrets unfurl,
While squirrels leap and branches twirl.
I overhear their playful schemes,
As sunlight spills in wavy beams.

The vines gossip with the breeze,
And tickle leaves, oh what a tease!
A hushed laugh, as shadows creep,
Those leafy dreams are mine to keep.

With rubies and emeralds, nature blinks,
While we exchange our joyful winks.
Together here, we spin a tale,
Of grassy paths where no one fails.

So come and join this leafy throng,
In bursts of green, we all belong.
With laughter wrapped in every shade,
Nature's rhythm is just displayed!

Green Whispers in the Canopy

Up in the trees, the gossip flies,
Squirrels share secrets, oh what a surprise!
The branches giggle, leaves sway in glee,
Nature's own drama, a leafy spree.

A parrot squawks tales, a rumor or two,
"Did you hear about the pine? It's feeling blue!"
The moss joins in with a chuckle so light,
As ferns shake their heads, "Oh, what a sight!"

Beneath the green canopies, laughter erupts,
Caterpillars dance, their diets corrupt.
With every breeze, the chatter grows loud,
A woodland party, join this leafy crowd!

So if you wander, just stop and lend ear,
To whispers of nature, sincere yet unclear.
For in every green corner, there's fun to be found,
In the world of the leaves, joy does abound!

Secrets Among the Leaves

In the thicket, whispers soft and low,
Rabbits share tales of a runaway doe.
The petals giggle as they dance in the breeze,
All sharing stories of life amongst trees.

The wily old fox with a grin on his face,
Speaks of the badger that fell flat on his face.
The daisies lean in, their heads bobbing wide,
As butterflies flutter, with nowhere to hide.

Under the branches, a secret life thrives,
Beetles playing poker, just counting their dimes.
The sun sneaks a peek; it's a raucous affair,
Even the shadows grin, enfolded in air!

So gather your wits and tune into the fun,
There's mischief aplenty before day is done.
Amongst all the leaves, let your laughter ring true,
The secrets are many, just waiting for you!

Verdant Truths Unveiled

In the garden of truths, plants uncurl and tease,
"Did you know daisies are experts at freeze?"
They poke fun at the roses, all prickly and sweet,
While violets whisper, "Let's feel the heat!"

The cacti chuckle, "We don't sweat a drop!"
While pansies laugh, "You've got quite the flop!"
The herbs mix their potions, concoctions they share,
With a dash of sarcasm, they fill up the air.

The spinach claims wisdom, ancient and bold,
As lettuce rolls eyes, "You're just getting old!"
Kale throws a party, a fiber-rich blast,
While mint brings the laughter, fresh and fast!

In this garden gala, let laughter be free,
Every plant a raconteur, come join the jubilee.
For beneath all the layers, there's humor to find,
Amidst verdant truths, let playfulness bind!

The Lush Heartbeat of Nature

The trees drum a rhythm, so deep and profound,
With roots tapping softly to a leafy sound.
Flowers sway gently, vibrate with cheer,
Each petal a giggle, for all to hear.

The river bubbles a pun, full of mirth,
As frogs leap around in a green, lively rebirth.
"Hey, can you croak it?!" one lily does tease,
While turtles just chuckle in slow, easy ease.

In the embrace of turf, laughter takes flight,
With crickets composing under soft moonlight.
The vibrant green hum, a symphony bright,
Nature's own orchestra, a true delight.

So if you are lost in this verdant domain,
Take heed of the laughter, it's hard to contain.
For in every rustle and bounce of the leaf,
Lies a heartbeat of joy, beyond any grief!

Fronds of Judgment

Amongst the leaves, I find a truth,
A gossiping fern with endless sleuth.
Whispering tales of the sun's bright glare,
While plotting revenge on the cloudy air.

A dandelion sneers at the oak's slow grace,
"Try growing hair, it'll give you space!"
The daisies giggle, a dance on the breeze,
Flaunting their colors with ridiculous ease.

Yet here I stand, in the green attire,
My leaves are sharp, and I never tire.
The grasses gossip, their secrets untold,
As mushrooms chuckle, both daring and bold.

So I leaf it all, with a flick and a grin,
To share in the fun of this garden din.
Each frond holds a secret, in silence they wait,
Until someone new swings the garden gate.

Metamorphosis of the Meadow

In a patch of wild flowers, things get bizarre,
A tulip claims it was once a star.
"See my petals? They shimmer and shine,
I danced with the cosmos, oh so divine!"

A beetle with swagger, he struts like a king,
Proclaims all the blooms are his endless fling.
"I transform the dull soil into pure delight,
With my charming good looks, I can turn day to night."

But the daisies are knuckleheads, too proud to confess,
Their puffy white heads in quite a mess.
They argue quite loudly, who leads the parade,
While the shy little violets just want to invade.

So here in the meadow, the laughter takes flight,
Each bud and each blossom, a whimsical sight.
With tales of transformation, they spin with glee,
In this secretive dance of the flora and me.

Toil and Tendrils

In the garden of giggles, I toil and bend,
Planting my dreams with a carefree trend.
The weeds laugh out loud, "You're wasting your time!"
As I water my hopes in this green pantomime.

With tendrils like spaghetti, they tangle my feet,
Comedic disasters, oh, they're such a treat!
The carrots are snickering, "Grow up, little sprout,"
While the radishes watch, with no hint of doubt.

And the tomatoes blushing, are sweet with a grin,
"Your garden's a stage, let the circus begin!"
So I juggle my watering can and hoe,
As the veggies perform in a row, in a show.

At dusk, when it's quiet, the moon casts a beam,
The critters are ready to join in my dream.
Toil and tendrils, a funny ballet,
In this thriving theater, we all sway and play.

Secrets Woven in Green

Deep in the forest, where giggles are found,
A squirrel tells secrets, all swirling around.
"Did you hear about the fern, who thought it could fly?
It dove off a rock, but oh my, oh my!"

The vines tell a tale of a caterpillar bold,
Who whispered sweet nothings to a marigold.
"Did you see it blush, in the warm summer light?
The blooms threw a party, what a curious sight!"

The moss, with a chuckle, sways to the beat,
Scanning the ground for the luckiest feet.
A chorus of laughter as flowers unite,
In this tangled-up world, the stars shine so bright.

So come join the ruckus, beneath leafy skies,
Where laughter and secrets are shared with the flies.
In this woven tapestry of giggles and glee,
The green confessions are waiting for me.

Lush Landscapes of Vulnerability

In a garden so green, I fell on my face,
Dancing with daisies, I lost all my grace.
The vegetables giggled, they knew my plot,
While I shouted at weeds, they just grew a lot.

The sun overhead was a sneaky old chap,
Burning my shoulders, I took a quick nap.
I dreamed of a salad, crisp, cool, and bright,
But woke to a pickle—my snack turned to fright.

The flowers were chuckling, I couldn't outrun,
As I slipped on a snail, it was all just in fun.
I told them my secrets, they swayed with delight,
While the carrots conspired to keep me in sight.

So here in this maze of green, lush and bold,
I laugh at my blunders, each story retold.
With leaves all around, I'll confess once or twice,
That growing with nature is worth every slice.

Breath of the Verdant Spirits

In a grove filled with giggles, the trees start to chat,
One said, 'I'm feeling a bit like a brat!'
With roots intertwined and laughter so free,
They whispered their secrets, just branches and me.

A squirrel joined the fun, with a nut in his stash,
He said, 'I'm the king, and I'm ready to crash!'
But tripping on acorns, he tumbled around,
Leaving all of us laughing, we rolled on the ground.

The ferns waved their fronds like they knew it was true,
That life in this jungle is never quite blue.
With laughter like petals fluffing up in the breeze,
We danced through the shadows, just vines and our dreams.

In this lively abode where green spirits blend,
We thrive on the chuckles that nature will send.
Each pause is a giggle, each gust brings a cheer,
Breathing in joy, in this playground we steer.

Leaves Like Letters on the Wind

Whispers in the branches, a letter's been found,
From leaves to the wind, it twirled round and round.
One wrote of a crush, a fern on a vine,
Another confessed, 'I'm just here for the wine!'

As gusts carried gossip from shrub to tall tree,
The blooms all perked up, 'Can you keep it a spree?'
With petals in pink, and a blossom in blue,
The news spread like wildflowers, laughter flew.

'I saw a snail race!' cried the lilac so bold,
'He slipped past my roots, it was purest gold!'
The mosses kept mum, while the daisies would shout,
Every leaf had a story, each one was a clout.

So here in the rustle of foliage divine,
Each whisper, a giggle, each silence—a sign.
With letters in breezes, a playful parade,
This playground of green leaves will never soon fade.

Treetop Testimonies

Up high in the treetops, I heard quite the scene,
A sparrow recounted her date with the green.
'He was such a catch,' she chirped with a sigh,
'But he left me for bait; you just can't trust a guy!'

The oak rolled his eyes, his bark full of zest,
'We all know that feeling; just count me the best!'
While the willow hung low with her long leafy hair,
She sighed, 'When you've branches, you just get the air!'

The gossip flowed freely as birds fluffed their feathers,
A chorus of truths intertwined with the weather.
Each twirl in the wind brought a chuckle anew,
Life's fibs and fables spin around like a stew.

So here's to the stories of this leafy retreat,
Where laughter and whispers find rhythm and beat.
With birds sharing tales and the breeze acting bold,
Treetop confessions are worth all the gold!

Beneath the Surface of Green

In the garden, greens conspire,
Tales of veggies, dreams of fire.
Lettuce giggles, sprouts unite,
Whispers float, a leafy sight.

Cucumbers plotting, sneaky schemes,
Radishes burst with juicy dreams.
Chasing bugs with frantic glee,
Nature's stage, a leafy spree.

Tomatoes blush beneath the vine,
Confessions made at dinner time.
Salad secrets, tossed around,
In this realm, joy knows no bounds.

Peas and beans, a clever joke,
While carrots laugh, they won't be broke.
Under the surface, life does flow,
In the green, the giggles grow.

Epiphanies of the Edges

Out in the wild, where mayhem thrives,
Foliage hosts hilarious lives.
A dandelion dreams of flight,
But gets stuck in a pollen fight.

There's a rogue vine with grand ideas,
Plotting to climb on passing dears.
Beneath the ferns, secrets abound,
Winks from nature, all around.

Grass blades gossip, sharing the tea,
About the squirrel's last fashion spree.
Branches sway, with laughter so bold,
In this green world, the stories unfold.

Mushrooms chuckle, lost in the sun,
While thistles tease, oh what fun!
Epiphanies dance at the edges,
Amongst the green, no one pledges.

Innermost Thoughts of the Thicket

Nestled deep in tangled dreams,
Where sunlight spills in joyful beams.
A twig declares, 'I'm quite the star,'
As shadows nod, from near and far.

Thickets whisper in playful tones,
Silly secrets, leafy groans.
The bushes chuckle in harmony,
While crickets join, a symphony.

Brambles boast their prickly reign,
Yet underneath, a giggly train.
Roots entwine with knowing grins,
In every corner, mischief spins.

Through the thicket, laughter roams,
Each fern holds tales of leafy homes.
Inner thoughts float, wild and free,
In this realm, nothing's just a tree.

Disguises in Green

In the meadow, all wear masks,
Grass blades posing as leafy tasks.
Every stalk, a hidden jest,
Camouflage, giving nature zest.

Pine trees whisper 'We're quite sly,'
As butterflies flit and gently fly.
The weeds are giggling on their thrones,
Pretending they're kings among the stones.

Frogs croak jokes from lily pads,
While hawks just laugh, they're wearing fads.
Caterpillars on a fashion spree,
Disguises bright as can be!

Nature's stage, a funny run,
Where every plant has jokes to stun.
In the wilderness where giggles blend,
Disguises in green never end.

Vines of Disclosure

Hanging around, I heard a plot,
The ferns they gossiped, in their own little spot.
"Did you hear what the ivy said?
He's climbing up walls, getting ahead!"

The tendrils giggled, twisting with glee,
"I saw her leaf dance, just wait and see.
The daisies rolling their eyes in suspicion,
What a tangled web of plant-based ambition!"

Buds popping jokes, under a bright sun,
"Your leaves are so green, but here's the pun:
If you're so fabulous, why hide in the shade?
Branches of laughter, memories made!"

So time flies by in this leafy affair,
Secret sunshine mingling with the air.
With roots in the ground, laughter takes flight,
Nature's comedy, blooming with delight.

The Conflicted Canopy

In the heart of the forest, trees squabble and shout,
"Why do these squirrels make such a rout?"
"Maybe they're plotting, with nuts for a crime,
Shushing the branches, is this a good time?"

"Look at the oaks, always somber and grand,
While we're up here, just trying to stand!"
"Maples throw shade, with their pompous displays,
But wait for fall, and they'll be all ablaze!"

Twigs are twisted, in frantic debate,
"Who has the best bark? This might seal our fate!"
Enter the willows, with their wispy tease,
"Let's sway with the winds and just aim to please!"

So amidst the drama, roots intertwine tight,
As laughter erupts in the dark of the night.
The canopy giggles, beneath the moon's glow,
Life in the treetops, hilariously slow.

Whispers of the Wilderness

In shadows and light, whispers float high,
"Did you hear what the wildflowers sigh?"
"Those bees are so bold, buzzing right through,
Claiming the blooms without asking 'who's who?'"

"Rabbits in huddles, gossip in fur,
Have you seen that fox? Such a furry blur!
Stealing a glance, thinking no one can see,
But I'm just a toad, splashing in glee!"

Swaying with laughter as the breezes conspire,
"Those butterflies dance, oh, they never tire!
With colors so bright, they steal every show,
Got us all laughing, so why not just glow?"

Amongst the tall grasses, secrets take flight,
With every soft rustle, nature delights.
Funny confessions, in the wild we reside,
Playing the game of 'who's that' with pride.

The Guilt of Lush Landscapes

Under the sun, the flowers complain,
"Too much rain and we're stuck in the lane!
The grass is so green, looks like we're all show,
But trust me, my roots, they crave some below!"

"Those daisies strutting, with petals on clear,
Think they're the best, oh dear, oh dear!
While the weeds are sneaking, thinking they're wise,
'We can grow anywhere!'—well, how about flies?"

A breeze brings buzz, as the trees shift and sigh,
"I missed the swipe of the sun, oh my!"
"Let's flip our leaves, join in this jest,
Admit we all sweat, despite being the best!"

As shadows stretch long, the laughter takes root,
In this garden of chaos, who needs the truth?
With petals and stems, their secrets entwined,
These guilty delights, in nature's design.

Emerald Echoes of the Soul

In a garden so lush, where secrets do sprout,
The daisies gossip, there's no room for doubt.
A sunbeam slips by, with a cheeky cheer,
"You can't plant your dreams, they're too dry here!"

The ferns start to giggle, the ivy rolls eyes,
"Did you hear that tale? It's quite the surprise!"
The tulips flip petals, sharing their glee,
"I traded my colors for a cup of green tea!"

As roots stretch their toes, they plot and they scheme,
"Let's throw a ruckus, we're living the dream!"
From seedlings to trees, they've got jokes to unfold,
The stories they share, worth their weight in gold!

Oh, nature, you sly, have a laugh with your friends,
In the leafy embrace, where the laughter transcends.
So dance with the breeze, let your spirit take flight,
In a world full of giggles, oh what a delight!

Confessions of the Forest Floor

Underneath the canopy, the pinecones conspire,
"Did you see the squirrel? He's caught in the wire!"
Mushrooms are chuckling, their caps up in glee,
"We're the party starters, just wait and see!"

The acorns are whispering, sharing their stash,
"I found a new home—it's a real leafy bash!"
The soil's got secrets, richer than gold,
"I've seen the wild stories of the trees being bold!"

A raccoon saunters by, with a wink and a grin,
"I'm just here to see what kind of trouble you're in!"
The ferns sway with laughter, their hands in the air,
"If plants had a band, we'd be rocking right there!"

So gather round roots, in the moss covered night,
Where whispers and chuckles take wonderful flight.
In this forest of humor, let joy unearth,
The delightful confessions of the soil's great worth!

Leafy Revelations at Dusk

As sunset draws near, the leaves start to chatter,
"Did you catch that bug? It thought it could flatter!"
With twirls and with sways, the branches do tease,
"We're the real stars here, don't you dare freeze!"

The shadows grow long, and the crickets do sing,
"Who knew the trees had a sense of bling?"
A rustle, a whisper, the vines share a tale,
"I once lost a twig on a treksome trail!"

The tulips are blushing, in colors so bright,
"Dance with us, petals, under the moonlight!"
The laughter cascades in the soft evening air,
Each leaf finds a partner, with jokes to share.

So embrace the dusk, let the frolic begin,
In the leafy confessions, where the stories spin.
With laughter still ringing, as day fades to night,
In this world of hilarity, everything feels right!

The Language of Living Green

In the heart of the garden, where laughter is found,
The daisies are chatting, spreading joy all around!
"Did you hear the one about the crow and the bee?"
"That bird has no style, just wait and you'll see!"

The sunflowers stand tall, with their heads held so high,
"I shine like a star, with no one to deny!"
With petals a-flutter, sharing tales with the breeze,
"What's the secret, dear sun? Is it all just a tease?"

A squirrel joins in, with a flick of his tail,
"I'm the funniest fella, with stories to regale!"
While the clovers all giggle, like whispers in green,
"Nothing blooms quite like laughter, you know what I mean!"

So let's raise a toast, with the juice of the vine,
To the language of green, where our worlds intertwine!
With each chuckle and grin, we spin through the day,
In this lively spectrum, we have so much to say!

Shadows of the Evergreen

Beneath tall trees, I often creep,
Where squirrels play, and shadows leap.
Their acorns stored, my secret stash,
I ponder life, then make a dash.

The leaves gossip, a lighthearted tune,
Swaying in rhythm to the sun's warm boon.
They laugh at me, a goofy sight,
Tripping on roots, in the soft twilight.

A pinecone's wisdom, it cracks a joke,
"You think you're wise? Just look at that oak!"
I chuckle back, quite proud and spry,
An evergreen laugh beneath the sky.

In this leafy world, where whispers flow,
Nature's jesters put on a show.
With every breeze, a snicker drifts,
Even trees have their funny gifts!

Nature's Silent Secrets

In the garden, mischief's brewing,
Petunias plot, the daisies skruing.
They nibble on sunlight, what a feast,
While the roses grumble, a floral beast.

A cactus stood, with barbed advice,
"Life's a prick—better think twice!"
Laughing roots engage in a fight,
Who knew plants could be such a sight?

With every bloom, a giggle's felt,
Lizzy the lark, she slyly dealt,
"I'm just a bird, in the breeze I play,
But you know your petals, they give me sway."

In the soil, secrets often lie,
Giggling worms, "We can't deny!
Life's a riot, beneath the earth,
Plant a seed, watch the laughter's birth."

Hushed Tales of the Botanical World

Underbrush whispers of secrets loud,
Ferns share tidbits that make them proud.
"Did you see the bee, with that silly buzz?
I swear it thinks it's one of us!"

A lilac shrugged, "I was once shy,
Until I learned to bloom and pry.
Now I tell jokes to every bee,
They laugh so hard, they drop their tea!"

Moss on the rock, a wise old sage,
Counts the ages from page to page.
"Life's a play, don't take the fall,
Just roll with it, and you'll have a ball!"

In this world where plants unite,
Each sprout and leaf ignites delight.
With laughter shared, their colors sing,
In nature's realm, joy's the spring.

When Foliage Speaks

When leaves start chattering on the breeze,
They giggle and chatter, doing as they please.
"Did you hear the tale of the wandering vine?
Thinks it's a fibber, oh what a line!"

A radish complained of its underground fate,
"Life's pretty dull when you're stuck in this state.
I want the spotlight, the glitz, the fame,
But here I am, just a root in the game!"

The oak retorted, "It's all in the grow,
You might surprise us if we see you glow.
Just sprout a joke and let the world in,
Who knew veggies had such a grin?"

So in this garden where laughter's made,
Every shade dances, every glimmer played.
Foliage speaks, in snickers and quips,
Plant a few smiles, and watch the world flip!

Unraveled Stories in Shades of Green

In the garden of gaffes, we sprout,
Tales of leaf-like laughter, no doubt.
With sunlight as our radiant guide,
We shimmy and shake, a green leafy ride.

From clumsy branches, pranks take flight,
Photosynthesis pun, oh what a sight!
The daisies giggle, the grass will play,
In the green, we find joy every day.

Chasing raindrops, we wiggle and sway,
In verdant chaos, we dance and play.
Nature's jesters in sunlight's embrace,
Even the weeds can't keep a straight face.

So come join the chorus, oh leafy friends,
In the meadow of mischief, where play never ends.
We'll whisper our secrets, with humor intertwined,
In this whimsical garden, joy's surely defined.

The Hidden Life Beneath the Surface

Beneath the soil, where the worms convene,
They plot a parade, quite a funny scene.
With roots that gossip and giggle so loud,
The fungi join in, all earthy and proud.

At midnight they dance, under stars so bright,
With snickers and chuckles, oh what a sight!
The beetles don tuxes, the ants wear a grin,
Their subterranean parties just make us spin!

Each root tells a tale, of mishaps and blunders,
In the underground world, where laughter just thunders.
With soil as their stage, the critters perform,
A comedic spectacle, quite far from the norm.

So if you should hear, a raucous delight,
Know it's the life down below, out of sight.
A hidden community, green chuckles they weave,
In the depths of the earth, they joyfully grieve!

Rooted Whispers of the Earth

In the quiet of roots, secrets abound,
With whispers of humor, they wiggle around.
They gossip about storms and playful winds,
While teasing the branches, and all of their sins.

The daisies eavesdrop, grinning with glee,
As the daisies inch closer, they join in the spree.
With every soft rustle, a joke starts to bloom,
In the rooted confessions, laughter fills the room.

Fungi flip jokes like pancakes at dawn,
In a world that's so wacky, where weirdness is drawn.
The earth's jesters giggle, as buds start to sprout,
In their rooted whispers, there's never a drought.

So tiptoe with joy in the garden of green,
Join the revelry where fun's evergreen.
In the depths of the soil, where shenanigans thrive,
It's the root of the laughter that keeps us alive.

Secrets Beneath the Bark

Underneath the bark, a party ensues,
With woodpeckers tapping, they share their news.
The trees tell tales of the squirrels' wild chase,
As beetles align with a smile on their face.

Each ring is a story, of laughter and glee,
The sap flows like soda, refreshingly free!
Old trunks crack jokes, while new shoots just beam,
In the forest of fun, it's a jovial dream.

Leaves chuckle softly as the breezes do tease,
The bark whispers secrets with mischievous ease.
With every rustling leaf, a punchline is born,
In the canopy of life, we laugh until morn.

So if you should wander where the tall trees dwell,
Listen closely for stories that bark will tell.
In the lush green theater, humor's in stock,
The secrets of nature tickle like a clock.

Nature's Silent Confessions

In the garden, plants conspire,
Whispering secrets of forest fire.
A daisy snickers, a tulip sighs,
While the shy ferns hide their lies.

The oak laughs loud, it's quite the show,
Bragging about its sap flow.
But roots are tangled, truth be told,
A little dirt can be quite bold.

The roses blush, with tales to weave,
Of insects flirting, oh, how they thieve!
Each leaf hides a giggle, oh so sly,
Nature's humor, always nearby.

A Symphony of Foliage

The leaves are singing, what a spree!
They love to dance and poke at me.
A breeze comes in, starts a laugh,
As branches sway, they take a bath.

Daffodils trip, oh what a sight,
Falling over in sheer delight.
The sunflowers gossip, heads held high,
Sharing tales beneath the sky.

With a crunching sound, the bushes will cheer,
As critters rumble, oh dear, oh dear!
The melody plays, it's quite absurd,
In this green theater, joy's preferred.

The Truths Beneath the Bark

Underneath, the whispers flow,
About the night and morning glow.
Bark-bound secrets, worn and wise,
Creaking tales of tree-top spies.

The squirrels scold, a nutty fight,
While limbs recount the leafy plight.
Each ring reveals another jest,
Years of laughter, quite the quest.

When rain starts falling, oh the chatter!
Leaves spill stories, miles of patter.
Beneath the bark, fun is raw,
Nature's giggles, with no flaw.

Confessions of the Forest Floor

Among the moss, the chatter grows,
As mushrooms gossip, in rows they pose.
With each fallen leaf, a tale unfolds,
Of critters creeping, and secrets bold.

The snails are slow, yet gossip fast,
Trading news that never lasts.
While beetles boast of hidden caves,
Their royal ways, but oh, how they rave!

A toad croaks jokes, quite the clown,
As leafy greens all settle down.
With laughter shared beneath the pines,
The forest floor is where fun shines.

In the Shade of Truth

In a leaf's green hug, secrets find,
Tell me your truth, don't be so shy.
Photosynthesized gossip, intertwined,
Under the branches, we giggle and sigh.

Plant puns and laughs, we thrive so bright,
Whispered in sunlight, from morn until night.
If roots had ears, oh what would they hear?
Laughs at the weather, while sipping a beer!

Try not to wilt under the green pressure,
The shade of the trees, our trusted treasure.
We chat about growth, with roots all around,
In our leafy haven, pure joy can be found.

So here's to the leaves, who know all our quirks,
Nature's wild whispers, with laughter it lurks.
Underneath the canopy's playful fold,
We tell our tales, oh so funny and bold.

Withering Secrets

Beneath the soil, where whispers fade,
The dirt holds tales of how we misplayed.
Dinner date with the sun; oh what a sight,
Sunned up and ready, we soared in delight!

Leaves taking notes on each other's slips,
When they spill their tea, it's a riot of quips.
Falling for gossip, like fruit from a vine,
Plucking the jokes, juicy and fine.

While petals blush from the sun's warm kiss,
They giggle and twirl in a dance of bliss.
Breezes carry laughter, spreading the cheer,
Join us in the whispers; come lend us your ear!

In nature's own way, we say what's absurd,
Leafy confessions, so candid, so stirred.
With hearts made of green, let's play and unite,
For even the verdant can be awkwardly bright.

The Lush Lament

In gardens where fables grow wild and free,
We moan 'bout the weeds, as they tickle our knees.
With roots in the gossip, oh can't you see?
The lush life is funny, just sipping our tea.

Petals complain of their beauty so bold,
"Oh my, the sun! It's too hot, I'm getting old!"
While vines twist around in their tangled embrace,
Their laughter erupts, a botanical race!

In the shade where the sprouts share their dreams,
We ponder connection, or so it seems.
Whirling and twirling, the fun never ends,
In this verdant confessional, we become friends.

So raise up your leaves, let the giggles spread,
For life is a garden, and laughter's the thread.
With laughter as soil, we flourish and bloom,
In a world where the green is forever in bloom.

A Tapestry of Turmoil

In dappled light, a tale unfolds,
Of plants in a panic, with secrets untold.
"We're wilting away! Must we grow up so fast?"
While giggles erupt from the roots that hold fast.

With stems that get tangled in dramatic flair,
Who knew that a plant could have so much to bear?
In this tapestry woven with laughter and sighs,
A patchwork of chaos, beneath the blue skies.

Leaves lean in closely, like friends at a chat,
Swapping their stories, oh what of that brat?
The bug that came sniffing, with mischief in tow,
A jester amoung us, stealing the show.

So here's to the garden, the hub of our strife,
Where each leafy whisper brings giggles to life.
In this vibrant collage, we dance and we jest,
A botanical chaos, where humor's the best!

www.ingramcontent.com/pod-product-compliance
Lightning Source LLC
Chambersburg PA
CBHW072215070526
44585CB00015B/1352